Power Guesting

Insider Secrets To Profit From Being A Great Podcasting Guest!

Heather Havenwood
Rob Anspach

Power Guesting
Insider Secrets To Profit From Being
A Great Podcasting Guest

ISBN-10: 0-9894663-8-8
ISBN-13: 978-0-9894663-8-7

Printed in USA

Disclaimer: Although the author and publisher have made every effort to ensure that the information in this book was correct at press time, the author and publisher do not assume and hereby disclaim any liability to any party for any loss, damage, or disruption caused by errors or omissions, whether such errors or omissions result from negligence, accident, or any other cause.

Dedication

To Joe Sugarman, thanks for everything!

Table of Contents

Foreword

By: Rob Anspach

Up until a few years ago I had no idea who Heather Havenwood was, or what she did. But we had the same mentor...Joe Sugarman.

So let me start there.

A month before I met Heather, I was sitting in a restaurant in Las Vegas having lunch with Joe. I was listening as Joe weaved one of his many stories and as he finished he said to me, "Rob, I would love for you to come to my event next month here in Vegas as my guest".

I was floored, excited, giddy and yes, even apprehensive. Here was my marketing hero asking me to come to his event. I replied, "Of course, tell me more!"

Joe explained that he partnered up with Heather and they were calling the event "The Success Magnet Seminar". I thought, hey that's cool, but who is Heather? Joe quickly put my mind at ease and told me about Heather and how she was spunky and sassy and had this new book called "Sexy Boss".

Well, I show up to the event and Heather was nothing like I pictured. Oh, she was all the things Joe said, but I also found her commanding, patient and very generous. Qualities that make a great coach, a fantastic leader and a successful entrepreneur.

And over the years we kept in touch via Facebook and the other social networks, and then one day she reached out to me for help.

Here, as it turns out, "Sexy Boss" the book Joe mentioned to me years ago was only available in digital Kindle and Heather, now after all these years, wanted it to be a real book. So with the wave of a hand and some magical marketing words I transformed the digital copy into a real book. Well, there was more to it than that, but throwing magic in there sounds cooler.

And that brings us to this book!

Although I helped, this book is mainly about Heather's adventures, her failures and her rise to success in the podcasting arena.

For those who wish to learn the art of being a powerful podcasting guest, this book will be your guide. And let me tell you, there is no other person to learn podcasting from than from Heather herself.

Enjoy!

Rob

Rob Anspach, founder
www.AnspachMedia.com

Introduction

By Heather Havenwood

Being invited as a guest on a podcast can be big boost to your sales. That's if you follow some guidelines. You see when you don't have a plan or adhere to what's prescribed from those who have been guests before, you won't know how to monetize your podcast experience.

And a bad podcast performance can cost you your reputation and diminish any authority as an expert you were trying to instill.

It's not rocket science, but there are tricks, tips, solutions and common sense examples that you should know prior to ever saying "yes" to being a guest.

That's where this book comes in. Welcome to Power Guesting. My goal is to help you become phenomenal at "guesting". That's the art of being a better podcast guest.

It wasn't always easy. I made mistakes. As you'll soon discover. But what I learned through failing, through being a guest on hundreds of podcasts and from having my own podcast show is that if you're not prepared, your presence will be noticed by the audience and you won't resonant with them nor will you be invited back.

But when done right, your presence on a podcast can shine, can add hundreds of new fans to your social following and make you the authority in your field.

Making sure your message, your story, your script is clear, to the point and that it does what you have envisioned it's supposed to do is just one of the many pro tips I share with you in this book. But your story and how you tell it, plays an important role in how you educate, entertain and engage your podcasting audience and get them to trust you, buy from you or join your list.

You ready to get started?

You ready to learn how to be a power guest?

Oh, and at the end of the book make sure you check out the resources and bonus offers.

Now turn the page and let's get you started.

Heather Havenwood
www.HeatherHavenwood.com

Chapter 1

The Low Hanging Fruit

Understanding What A Podcast Is

Now, for those who don't understand what podcasting is, or the benefit of being on a podcast, let me explain. In a nutshell, it's sharing your story through conversation with a group of people that might be hundreds or even thousands of miles away. Or even across the globe.

Typically, a podcast is where one person interviews another in 15-45 minute segments which is then uploaded to a service so others can listen right away or download for future listening via iTunes, Stitcher, Google Play and others.

Unfortunately, my first venture into podcasting failed. But I learned some very valuable lessons, which I'll share with you. It was in early 2013 and my podcast show was called the Sexy Boss Show and sadly it was aired in the graveyard section. I think it's still out there somewhere…if you go look for it. But, honestly I didn't know what I was doing. I didn't understand the medium of it all, of what podcasting really meant. And yes, there is a particular medium of podcasting.

Maybe you tried podcasting too? And if you're

reading this book, you probably want to know how to improve, because just like me your first venture into trying podcasting most likely didn't end up successful.

The thing I learned quickly about podcasting, which I got this from my friend Alex Mandossian and Paul Colligan, it is all about the "low hanging fruit". Which I didn't understand at first, but the more I listened to Alex the more I got it. It was this simple approach that opened my eyes to how I could be better at podcasting and ultimately teach you how to be better as well.

The low hanging fruit...is audio! What? You thought I was going to say something else? Audio is one of the those few remaining mediums that allows you to go anywhere and just listen. With iTunes and your iPhone or MP3 player or mobile device you can download audio apps and listen on the go. Mobility and On-Demand is the key.

This becomes that low-hanging fruit. Audio can go with you where you go. In your car, walking down the street, on a plane, while on a cruise or even in jungle...that's the beauty, you could be traveling anywhere and you can still listen. You can download an episode and take it with you. So if you don't have Wi-Fi, because you're on the beach or high in the sky on a plane or walking through a rainforest you can still be listening to something. Yep, listening!

Audio allows us to listen while we're enjoying life. Video doesn't always do that.

Yup, that low-hanging fruit is audio. Not video.

That's a beauty of this medium. With podcasting it's about storytelling and conversation. In the world of, let's say TV interviewing, interviewing is very short. If you've ever been prepped by a public relations firm or PR person, your interview time is three to five minutes. Maybe seven if you're a presidential candidate. It's quick, quick, quick. Get in, get interviewed, and out you go. It's like speed dating. They just want tips, facts but not necessarily a full story.

Podcasting is different. It's your chance to slow it down a little bit and enjoy the time.

You're in it for the conversation.

It's about you sharing your story.

It's you connecting to the world and sharing what you do. What your company does and why they do it.

It's entertainment. It's education. It's storytelling.

No speed dating here…this is you on a deeper level.

You get to connect with the audience as the expert.

Podcasting is that "go anywhere" medium that allows you to basically give an interview with anyone, anywhere from the comfort of your kitchen table while drinking your morning coffee. Imagine that! You give an interview today about how you and why you started selling your unique handbags online…and someone halfway around the world is downloading that interview onto their digital device and listening to you while they walk the streets of Florence, Italy looking for their next leather crafted handbag. Sale! Bam! Kind of cool, huh?

But if you rely on a typical Public Relations firm…podcasting usually doesn't fit into the agenda.

Remember speed dating?

Regular PR people have a hard time with podcasting because they train their clients that their job is to... answer questions fast. And then you're done.

With podcasting, you get to broaden your answers. You get to share your story. It's no longer a soundbite. It's you sharing your life, your experience, your talents, your pain and allowing others to learn from you.

It is way more intimate than radio.

It really is a conversation.

Here is an interview I did with Jessica Rhodes about the difference of regular PR and podcasting.
http://heatherhavenwood.com/tag/the-win-podcast-jessica-rhodes/

Sometimes that conversation is between you and the host (the one doing the podcast) and sometimes it's between a group of individuals brought together to share a common theme.

It's usually one-on-one. It is more intimate.

But I've had a few when the podcast became more like a party.

I like to hear podcasts when the interviewee or interviewer brings their friend or partner along. You get to hear multiple perspectives. And when it's me on the actual show as a guest, wow...I get to be interviewed by both of them. It is like this huge dinner party with friends So much fun.

It's way different than radio, one of the main ways is that you get to expand and go into your personal story so that people really understand you and your story of your business.

I think one of the biggest challenges to podcasting is the storytelling. Yup, there's a lot of storytelling and if you don't know how to crack the story, then you're missing out.

Did you ever talk to somebody who doesn't know how to tell a story and you're just bored out of your mind?

You have to learn how to share your personal story so that it's entertaining and yes, there's an art to it.

I think Joe Sugarman is by far one of the most brilliant storytellers ever.

For those that don't know…Joe is the founder of BluBlockers (probably the greatest sunglasses on the planet) and just one heck of a fantastic marketer, oh, and a super nice, sweetheart of a guy too!

Just phenomenal stories he has. He could tell the same story over and over again and it's always fascinating to listen to them. I'm sure you know great storytellers like Joe, right?

I've heard him tell the same stories at least five or six times and it never gets old. Why? I think it's how he presents those stories. Whether sharing one to one or in a group of 200 or more…even though I've heard the story before, once you get sucked into the story, you just want to hear it all over again.

I asked Joe once, "Don't you get tired of sharing the same stories?"

And he's like, "No, because no one really gets

tired of hearing the same stories."

There's always a reason to it.

Joe always makes a lesson of the story.

Joe explained it to me something like this…here it goes… "There's a reason I'm telling you this like a story. It's a lesson of success and sometimes failure and of life. You will always remember the story."

One of Joe's famous stories which goes back to the late 1960's involves Batman. And if you ever get the chance to hear Joe tell this story grab a chair and just listen. For the story is a good one. And, although the story is only about 15 minutes long…it certainly seems longer.

Those who have seen Joe speak or have heard him tell the Batman story always remember it. Always.

You see, that's the beauty of podcasting you can share your story (even if you only have one) to many audiences over and over again. If it's a good story it'll never get old. And, the audience will remember and connect with you and your story.

Repeating The Story

I learned from Joe Sugarman (as I previously shared) and also from another brilliant marketer named Dan Kennedy about the power of telling the same stories. It becomes an art form. It becomes your presentation. Your way to pull listeners in, so they want to know more and eventually hire you to help them.

My journey to discover how I could use storytelling as my presentation took time…and was in essence an evolution of my own learning process. It took seven years.

In the end, I learned the art of presentation skills and storytelling from traveling the country for years, with great speakers and presenters that knew their stories backwards and frontwards, inside and out. Their stories became their script. Yes, their script.

It was 2001 and we were doing the same presentation twice a day, three times a week, every week, 50 weeks a year. I don't know the exact number of presentations we did, but it was a lot. And yes, it was the same presentation over and over again. And the same stories over and over again.

Now, you would think these speakers and presenters would be exhausted of their stories but the more they shared it, practiced it and scripted it, the more powerful the stories got...until...they would tweak things.

Maybe if we moved that part here instead, or added a word there or deleted that phrase. And so it went...the stories were the same...just the script changed making every presentation better. Slight tweaks here and there.

Although they would tweak things, they wouldn't change it unless they really felt it wasn't converting well. By converting, I mean producing sales. If only 10% of the audience was buying the script would be adjusted to try to get 20%, 30% or more consistently buying. Big Money!

Same thing goes for podcasts.

You're going to share the same stories over and over again, tweaking the script ever so slightly to improve the message. To improve the conversion.

Think of your scripts as verbal copywriting. Your audience may not be able to see the words such as in a printed advertisement or Video Sales Letter, but they can hear your message and be drawn in by the stories.

I've done over 200 podcasts and although I don't know who is listening I'm pretty much consistent on my stories. It doesn't matter if someone listened to me twice on two different podcasts or subscribed to multiple shows that I appeared on or that their audiences were of varied subjects. It just reinforces my message to them.

Look at politics. Look at all the other people that are constantly sharing their stories. They say the same thing over and over again.

How many times must people have to hear something? To get in their head. To remember it.

How many times have you shared your story?

Sharing your stories across many podcast shows helps you perfect your script and allows you to become more known in many circles.

Chapter 2

Sharing & Converting

How Copywriting Influenced Podcasting

Back in the day, well in my case in the 1990's and early 2000's was sort of a turning point in my understanding of how marketing, especially copywriting, could be used to promote a product while attracting the right audience.

This type of copywriting was being used to promote the event marketing space. You know, "getting butts in seats!" I had the privilege of working with Ron LeGrand, The Robert Allen Institute, Ted Thomas and Marshall Sylver...just to name a few. These guys basically laid the groundwork for many to follow.

Yeah, I got to work alongside these great masters. It was these guys who introduced me to copywriting. And how copywriting is really the art and science of sales through words and presentations. Sound familiar? It's a way to tell a story to compel someone to take action.

These early mentors were the ones that got me excited and interested in marketing. I realized then that everything is a sales copy. Everything you do from the tweet, to the Facebook post, to the emails you send, to the podcasts you're on...it's you creating a compelling reason for someone to buy from you. Or to take an action towards a yes.

In 2009, I built a business from scratch called datingtriggers.com. This was basically a website filled with brilliant copywriting which focused on helping men learn the secrets to dating women. It is based on a simple premise and everything is done via email.

I got so great at email copywriting that it became a science. Every email I treated as just another way to improve my copywriting skills. My good friend John Carlton shares this saying in many of his talks, "If you want to get really good at copywriting, you have to write every day." Yes, every day!

And every day I would write 3 maybe 4 of these copywriting emails.

It was that daily exercise of writing that lead me to creating the Sexy Boss book and then launching my own event with Joe Sugarman called Success Magnet Seminar. It gave me that defining moment and of my declaring "Hey, this is what I am. This is what I'm doing. I want to empower other people to understand the art and science of copy and how it can really change their life."

You're probably wondering how this copywriting stuff helps with podcasting, right?

To most people copywriting is thought of as words in print. A sales letter, an article, maybe even some fancy website.

Think of podcasting this way...it's a just a medium. Just like the sales letter or the article or the website but instead of written words you have vocal words. It's your speech. That script we talked about. That compelling personal story you share.

It's you sharing your experiences, your life, your reason why your started your business to your potential clients. Just like Robert Allen would do in his seminars, you are doing via a podcast. It all comes down to moving someone from where they're at to an experience through education, entertainment and a call to action. It's less about the content and more about the experience.

Converting Your Message

Those stories that we talked about, that script that you rehearse time and time again...it all needs to do one thing…convert. Yep, conversion is the key piece. No matter what I'm doing, I'm always thinking about conversion. What's my intention? What am I trying to accomplish? Do I want more traffic to my website? Do I want more sales? What is the goal? Is the goal an opt-in? Or maybe a download?

So it comes down to making sure your message, your personal story, your script is clear, to the point, and that it does what you have envisioned it's supposed to do. Convert!

There's two elements in podcasting that I want to bring to your attention. So the next time you're invited to be a guest on a podcast to share your story, you're prepared.

The first element is knowing your audience. Who are they? Who's listening? Make sure your story resonates with them. You don't have to have new stories or deviate from telling them, you just need to make sure your story about you, your business, your vision is in alignment with your audience.

The second element is connecting to that audience. I want to make sure that everything I'm saying is landing (or connecting) with the right people. Whether it's a female audience, a male audience, those in their 20's, 30's, 40's, 50's or even 60's, 70's and older. I might change a little bit of the story to connect better. My goal is to be in their world, in their mind, thoughts and their life. I keep the conversations anchored around the theme of the podcast, but I tweak it here and there to resonate better with the listener.

Most podcasts are designed around a certain niche. So understanding what that niche is and how you can solve their problems or biggest challenges by educating their audience is a big plus. Say, the podcast you want to be on is highly spiritual, can you still talk about business? Sure, as long as your message is softer on the business aspect and is geared to help them understand the dynamics of how spirituality connects to business. Pushing a product on most podcasts is generally frowned on. Now, if you were on a business podcast, and you wanted to push your products and services, ask the host first if it's okay to do so.

So the "tell me more about your podcast" question helps you solve the mirror match and understand the audience you will be sharing your experience with.

One thing I do as a guest prior to recording the podcast. I always ask the host this one major question.

"Tell me more about this podcast!"

This opens the door for the host to share who the audience is, the goal of the show and gives me the best direction to take as their guest.

Chapter 3

Possibilities Happen

Being Open To The Possibilities

Some people get on a few podcasts and feel great about themselves and think they are doing great. To me a few doesn't really cut it. I've gone above and beyond. And opened myself up to the possibilities of all kinds of different podcasts. From August 2015 to early 2017 I've been on close to 200 different podcasts.

Is there one I favor over the others? Is there one niche I feel more comfortable helping?

No, not really, I'm really open. I've been on a lawyer's podcast. That was fun! I've been on a doctor's podcast. I've been a guest on marketing and sales podcasts, dog owner's podcasts, sales podcasts and even a podcast designed for actors.

There's a podcast on just about anything nowadays. The key is learning who the market is, the niche and how you can help them with the challenge or problem they are up against.

Previously, I talked about the dynamics of speaking on a spirituality podcast, and there's some pro's and con's to it so I want to share with you my thoughts. The only podcasts I tend not to say yes to anymore are the ones with a strong faith and political based messages. You see, I'm very strong in my own faith and political views and I just don't want to lead with politics or religion. It's just not the market for me. I'd prefer if asked, to go on the show and talk about the sales and marketing perspective to faith-based leaders and politicians. To teach them how to use marketing, copywriting, storytelling and sales techniques to attract their audience and increase donations.

To me the subject of sales and marketing can be applied to most podcasting niches.

One person who made a career out of speaking to faith-based audiences is Dave Ramsey. He takes his financial message to the masses (no pun intended). His scripting, his stories and his presentations all center around helping people grow stronger in their faith, while at the same time overcome the notion that "money is the root of all evil". Money is just a tool. It can be used in good ways and bad ways.

I had a gentleman contact me who dismissed the notion that his audience needed my help as he replied to me… "I don't think we can give you a shot, our podcast is for actors".

My response was… "What do you think actors are? They are entrepreneurs promoting the heck of themselves. I would love to talk to them on how to promote themselves on LinkedIn and how to get more acting jobs."

He was like…
"Oh, okay, that's cool!"

Keep an open mind. By saying "YES" to enough podcasts you will get experience needed to know who your niche market is and why. Plus, you will feel more comfortable knowing which podcasts to turn down, or to go after.

Being open to the podcasting possibilities doesn't necessarily mean you say "YES" to them all. It all comes down to how you resonate with that niche and your integrity level.

Yes, I did say integrity!

Integrity is the thing that needs to be constant in your life. If you say one thing to one audience yet, say the very opposite to another audience…not only aren't you believing a word you say, but the audience will catch on and not believe you either. Your character will be destroyed and you won't be invited back.

In today's fast paced social media world, it only takes one person to feel you don't have integrity to post a negative comment and the next time you know you're in damage control mode. Having integrity is just that important.

Everything Happens For The Best

After my Sexy Boss Show podcast failure. You know the one with like 2 subscribers which aired on the graveyard shift. I told you this story right? Oh, it was a massive failure. The concept was excellent, my understanding of podcasting at the time wasn't. That podcast died very quickly. It was at that time that my mentor Joe Sugarman said these words that changed my perspective on life…

"Everything happens for the best…not a reason…but for the best!"

He went on to share with me, "Heather, if you look for the reason then you'll also look for the why.

Don't look for the reason, go past the situation and trust that it happened for the best."

There's a lot of why's there, don't you think? That's exactly the point. Too many of them. When you look for a reason you look for the all the why's of what made that reason happen. You over analyze. You think it to death.

Yes, my podcast was a failure. And I was depressed. I wanted to know all the reasons why it failed. I questioned everything. And, it became a cycle of going round and round trying to understand why my podcast didn't do what it was supposed to do.

Joe's message cleared my mind of all the questions. The podcast failure was there to teach me a valuable lesson. There doesn't have to be a reason. It is what it is. It happened. Let's move forward.

And so armed with my new perspective on life...my attitude changed.

Although leery of doing my own podcast again, the notion of being a guest seemed like a natural fit. I didn't have to stick to one format. I could pick and choose what podcasts I wanted to be a guest on. Instead of trying to build my own audience. Being a guest allowed me to tap into other people's different audiences. To share my stories, my struggles, my experiences with a multitude of niches.

Yup, it really was for the best.

I just didn't see the potential in the failure. I was looking for the why...which, was the wrong thing to be thinking about.

My goal now turned to getting on as many podcasts that match my integrity and that I can add as much value, entertainment and education as I possibly can. So when the podcast announcer stops recording and says "That was great, I can't wait to publish this!"

Or when the podcast is supposed to come out (publicly launched) in six weeks, yet they email you and say, "I'm moving it up to next week, because we love it".

When you come from a mindset of adding value to others it changes how your stories flow, how your scripts are written and how people perceive your experiences. Yes, always in the forefront of your thinking, when it comes to podcasting is... add value, add value, add value.

That's how I went from failure at my own podcast to being a guest on almost 200 podcasts in less than a year.

Think about that for a moment – say it is 200 podcasts I've been on. And say each podcast is heard by 1000 people, that's over 200,000 people that have heard my story.

Now, let's say for the sake of those statistic geeks out there. The one's who like to see the numbers...if 1% of those 200,000 people took action and went to your website or social page or bought your book or called you, you'd have 2000 followers.

But if you get on a podcast and have the attitude of "It's all about me" and "talk about me" there's no value there. Then sadly, those numbers above won't mean diddly squat, because you won't be invited back.

My job is to entertain them, to add value to their life. Not sell them. It's definitely the difference between radio and podcasting. Radio is like, "My name is…this is my book…go find me on…I got to go." No value, just a quick sound bite.

Final thoughts:

Everything happens for the best.

Chapter 4

Overcome Your Fear

It's Okay To Be Scared...Just Improv It!

Entrepreneurs get scared...I get it. They're scared to get behind the microphone or the camera. They're scared they will mess up, fail, falter, stutter, or completely botch their stories. Success happens because of failure. Hey, if I can do it so can you.

I'm going to give you 5 ways to overcome that feeling of being scared...ready?
1. **Learn the principals**
2. **Being really present**
3. **Say yes**
4. **Know what your intention is**
5. **Enjoy the flow of the conversation** – don't try to control it.

Okay let's break them down so you have an idea what they all mean and how you can benefit.

Remember, everything happens for the best!

Three years ago, I walked into a local Improv class. You know improvisation. The stuff they do on some of those comedy TV shows. Well, I was depressed and I wanted to do something out of my comfort zone. Even my coach was saying, "Heather, do something out of your space. Do something where you don't know anyone, go bowling or something really weird for you." Hah, I guess she had me pegged, but bowling...nope!

At that time, I lived up the street from this huge theater in Austin. They taught improv. I didn't even know what it was. I thought, "okay, I'm going to go there". No one I knew was there. It was totally out of comfort zone. So there I was literally walking into some class, paid some strangers money to teach me and I really had no clue what it was I was signing up for...just for the sake of getting my butt out of the house.

It turned out, I was good at it.

A year went by, and I had taken every course they had offered. They actually had to kick me out. Not in the physical sense but the proverbial one. The instructor was like, "We don't have any more classes for you, Heather."

So there you have it, I learned the principals. It takes time. And sometimes it takes you on a journey of discovery. One that gets you out of your comfort zone and into a new space.

Improv at least for me helped make my copywriting better, my stories became more dynamic and gave me the ability to think faster in the moment while on podcasts. With improv there's no scripts. It's the opposite of acting. It's the ability to be in the moment and to feed off that moment.

Of course, podcasting is all about being in the moment. And sometimes it takes discipline and improv to keep the pace moving so the audience sticks around.

If you try to control the interview, it'll get really weird fast. So being really present will allow you to slow it down a bit and listen to the host. If you want to talk about business and the host wants to know more about your kids…it's just not going to go over well. Unless you loop it in. Yes, I said loop it in. It's when you have a subject that you might be passionate about but someone else wants to know something different. We loop one subject into the next. "Okay, great… did your kids help you with your business?"

Looping helps. Trying not to control the conversation…that helps too!

Well number three is actually a principle of improv, it's called saying "YES AND!" As in… "YES DEAR"! The way to save a relationship or keep a marriage intact. Or, to keep something moving along.

The principal of YES AND is whenever someone comes to you with something you just say, "Yes...And let's talk about... (those policies, the rules, the game, the alien to your left).

An example might be... the host wants to talk about my first book, but I want to bring up my newest and upcoming book, so I might say, "yes that was a great book, and this new book I wrote expands on the premises and gives people a better understanding of this..."

It's about moving the conversation to where you want it to go. You are not controlling just guiding a little here and there.

Yes...And...

Know who you are talking about and know who your host is. Be in their world. Understand them. Be present.

As a guest being present means to know what the intention of the show is and what ideas you want to cover and talk about. Make sure you know what the audience is hungry for, and how you can help them. Remember, it's a conversation between you as a guest and the the host of the show. It's not a sales presentation. You don't talk down to people. You educate, entertain and engage them.

Remember, it's a conversation. Enjoy it.

Even though your primary thought is to somehow grab an extra sale or have the audience go to your website or convert someone to a follower on your social page...the main purpose of a podcast is to share your story with the audience.

The host engages with you so you in turn can educate and entertain their listeners, you are a guest in their home. It's a mutual symbiotic relationship. You know your stories in and out, back and forth but without the host and their show to share them with, the audience will never learn about you. The better you are at scripting your stories around a conversation the better outcome you will have for the host to produce a great show. And the better chance you'll get invited back or the hosts recommend you on other podcasts.

So, stop being scared and improv it. Learn the principals, be really present, say Yes...And, know what your intentions are and enjoy the conversation.

You Got Invited...Now What?

So you've been invited on a podcast and you're nervous you might mess up, do you ask for the questions in advance or pray they don't ask something embarrassing?

Well, there's two schools of thought here...the first being that you want to be prepared, and the second is that you are curious as to what the questions are and if you are allowed to change them in any way. I get it, you don't want to mess up. You don't want to appear dumb or stutter when a question is posed that you don't know the answer to. Face it, knowing the questions before hand gives you a slight advantage doesn't it?

Well, yes and no!

The more prepared you are, the more shortened your answers become. A question posed in advance is usually answered methodically, it's planned, with no emotion and very little inflection. It's like you studied the answer to quickly shout it out.

I find prearranged questions kill off the podcast and make it boring for the listener. The questions aren't always broad enough to get you to elaborate. Then the host is scrambling to pull more from you to fill time. Not very entertaining or fun!

A prearrange question might be "What are the five books you like?" And, you just rattle off the titles without going into detail why those 5 books mean anything to you.

"One, two, three, four, five", nope no feeling there.

But, I'm thinking, "Ah", it's a checklist, so what kind of value does that add?

Maybe had they asked, "what's the one tip you can give the listener right now that could really help their business". The answer wouldn't be so robotic as one, two, three, four, five.

And instead of just blurting out a one-word answer saying what the one tip is, you would expand on that and talk for about 5 minutes sharing a story on how that one tip saved your business from failing.

Let's say your pre-arranged question was, "What's the one thing you need to implement right now in your business?" And you answer, "Email marketing".

Now the host wants to know more and says, "well, what does email marketing mean?"

Then it finally hits you that maybe you should go into more detail, duh! Okay, "Let me explain to you five tricks you can implement into your business using email marketing that will increase profit."

Now instead of prearranged questions that really doesn't make the host or the guest sound enthusiastic...try relaxing and taking a deep breath before getting on the podcast and just being yourself. Unprepared but determined. Improv it!

I know it sounds crazy...but honestly, with close to 200 podcasts to my name, as a guest, I think I know a tad bit of what works and what doesn't work.

If for some reason you still have a fear of being asked questions off the cuff, that's perfectly okay. But understand, you want to come across as your authentic self.

Final Thoughts:

Yes…And

Be Present

Be Your Authentic Self

Improve It.

Chapter 5

Promote, Promote, Promote

Sharing Your Audio Business Card
(Guest Podcast)

You were invited on a podcast, you shared your stories and the host and audience just loved it. Great. Now what? This is the part of the book where I tell you to promote, promote and promote. To which, you're probably just staring at the page thinking I hope she goes into detail about the whole promote thing, because I haven't got a clue. Right?

Of all the podcasts I was on, I promoted them. Yes, every single one. Why? It's simple...I'm on them. And I want others to know more about me. Each podcast is a unique audio business card that I can share. It's an audio business card where I share my story, add value and promote myself. Why would I not share?

You see every podcast I've been a part of is not only promoted by the host or hosting company, but it's shared all over their social media for their audience to listen to anytime, anywhere. Yup, shared everywhere. I love it! You should too!

Which means every podcast gets its own unique web link and its own audio file to download. That audio file can then be added to your website to help you showcase the show and demonstrate to people your authority.

Let's say you were invited on a TV show operated by a big television network and you think it's a huge deal. It is! You should take advantage of it. I was guest on a NBC affiliate TV morning show which was super awesome, by the way, and yes, I promoted the crap out of it. Why wouldn't I right? It's NBC!

They are talking about me. Why would I not tell everybody I know that I was on NBC?

Just the other day I was on a lawyer podcast.

You might be thinking okay, "yeah whatever...a lawyer podcast". Maybe not as glamorous as being on NBC TV. But, here's the lesson...just because it's a big name doesn't mean you will automatically generate a response.

I promote all my podcasts and TV spots equally.

I promote because I never know which one is going to be the one that generates a response from a listener that day or week or even months out. You just never know.

Back to the lawyer podcast...I got an email from an attorney who happened to catch the podcast after I shared it on my Facebook. He sent an email it read...

"Hey, Heather I was listening to the "Practicing Wealth for Lawyers" podcast, could you help me with my practice?"

And that's how it's done!

With me so far?

What about your email list?

Can you share your podcasts with them?

You betcha!

Maybe you have list of email subscribers or a list of subscribers to your e-newsletter that haven't responded in a while. Sharing your podcast (the audio business card) is a perfect way to bring them back into your funnel again.

Promoting a podcast, you were a guest on is such a great way to convert leads to take action. I've had people on my email list for years reach out after hearing a podcast and say, "Wow, that was awesome. I had no idea you had such experience at email marketing, can you help me in my business?"

Sometimes people forget what you do. Entrepreneurs especially. A podcast reminds them of what you know and how you can help them. Remember it's that audio business card...your audio business card.

Those podcasts need to be shared. Tell your fans, friends and followers. Share those podcasts on Facebook, Twitter and LinkedIn. Take a screenshot of the website the podcast is on and share that picture to Instagram and Pinterest. If you can download the podcast, make sure you upload it to your YouTube channel for even more exposure.

Share, share, share!

Oh, and don't forget about adding it to your own website. Create a page just to showcase all the podcasts you were on. It's all about promotion. It's all about building authority with your audience. And, connecting with them.

Your Time...Their Money!

Podcasts are totally different then the "Pay to Play" model of television and radio. If you were to pay for an ad or infomercial on TV or radio the costs would be astronomical. But being a guest on a podcast...is usually free or a lower cost. Just your time.

But here's the thing...the podcast producer/host incurs the production costs. He or she needs to pay people to create the marketing for the podcasts, they need to create thumbnail pictures for the videos and images to share on social media. Then they also have to pay the audio editor to go over the podcast and clean it up. Let's say for the sake of argument that each podcast costs $200 (it's honestly probably more). But $200 seems like a good number.

You as a guest don't have to pay that. You were invited to share your wisdom, your experiences, your joys, fears and failures so others could learn. So essentially you are being gifted $200 in free advertising just for your time.

Just imagine…an hour of your time dedicated to telling the world all about you and it doesn't cost you a quarter as much as TV or radio. And, all the artwork is created for you to share.

Let's compare a little bit shall we. If you were granted the same $200 credit to use say on Facebook Ads or Google Adwords would you get the same results as one hour of podcast time? How about a $200 credit in your local newspaper?

You have to think of it that way.

Being a guest on a podcast is a paid advertising medium. You are paying with your time and a lower cost placement instead of a larger amount of money. That's why when you are on a podcast your job is to give lots of value. The more value the more the host of the podcast is going to want to promote you. The more promotion the better chance you attract new clients. The more new clients the more growth and profit!

So an hour of your time is worth what? $100, $200, $500 or more?

Yes, time is money. But how do you leverage that time to maximize the return on your invested time? The answer would be...podcasts, duh! That's what this whole book is about.

It's a trade off...your time...their money. In return, you get traffic to your website, social pages, email lists and more. So that one hour of time could potentially generate you more than that $100, $200, $500 per hour you typically charge.

So the next time you think, "What am I doing this for?" You need to realize it's not just to hear yourself...it's about traffic...it's about leads...and it's about profit.

Final Thoughts:

Getting traffic to your company's website costs money, leverage your time and other people's money by being a great guest and giving value on other's podcasts.

Chapter 6

It's All About Failure

Talk About Your Failures

Yeah, I know it's not a comfortable subject for some people. But let's talk about failures. Joe Sugarman said it right. "Failures are life lessons and some are very comfortable talking about them and others are not." What gets me is all the entrepreneurs who refuse to learn from or share their past mistakes. They continue to try new things but never get to the root of why things keep failing for them. They don't acknowledge their mistakes and never learn from the failures.

If you're reading this then you want to know all about podcasting, because… well, you either failed at or don't want to fail at it. Either way you are acknowledging that you need help.

You see, I failed. I failed a lot. I failed more times than I succeeded. Joe Sugarman talks a great deal about failing. And let me tell you, you talk about failing big…listen to his stories and you'll know what I mean. He lost millions. As he tells it, one success can wipe out all those failures overnight.

Joe was the first person in my life, mentoring me, that really gave me full permission to fail. Later on an old friend of mine in the real estate field said,

"You've got to learn to fail forward fast". When he told me that I was like, "What does that mean?"

Fail forward fast?

Never heard of that before. But growing up I heard the opposite very frequently.

If you think back to kindergarten or first grade, whenever you started elementary school, what did they say? "Don't fail kindergarten or you won't make it to first grade. Don't fail first grade or you won't go to second grade. Don't fail second grade or won't head to third grade." And so on. That mindset <u>not to fail</u> is ingrained in us at a very young age. We are taught to win. You always have to win or you don't get to go along with everybody else.

Hah, but being an entrepreneur is different.

Being an entrepreneur is the culmination of failure.

You are told to fail, fail, fail, fail, fail then you'll succeed.

Failing is not having a victim mentality. Not if you're an entrepreneur. There is no room for that thinking.

Sure there's a fear of looking bad. A massive fear. I've had that!

I've had it for years.

That fear of looking bad slapped me right in the face one day when I went through my personal bankruptcy and my massive house foreclosure. It was horrible. I cried for months.

I remember being on the phone with Alex Mandossian, crying my eyes out and yes, I did pull the "I'm a victim" stuff on him. He replied, "One day, you're going to write a book about this."

Of course, I didn't believe him. And, I cussed him at him, saying "No, I will never share this. Ever". I felt embarrassed by my failure. I had lost everything. I didn't want anybody to see what was going on. I didn't want them see my bruises, my torn ligaments or my skinned knees. I really wasn't physically broken just mentally off. I had let myself down and I felt I let others down as well.

With Joe's help in being a mentor I turned my embarrassing failure into a book. Sexy Boss is actually my book about my failures and how I rose from the ashes. It was my story and although I wrote the book for me, it has benefitted so many men ns women. It felt so good to get those failures out and into the open that they no longer had power over me. I was free to share them with all who wanted to know.

Once I got the book and started to share the stories of failure on podcasts and in seminars and saying, "Yeah I failed". People would respond, "Oh, me too!"

Failure is actually the gift that keeps on giving. It's also the gift that when you share it, people understand, they have compassion and connection. Failure is the ultimate life lesson.

Now if you're one of those people who falls for those email pitches or fancy webinars about how to be successful let me share something with you...if they aren't showing you their failures then don't believe them.

The guy is living in a 50-million-dollar mansion, driving a 5-million-dollar exotic sports car and the whole ad is encouraging you to buy whatever the product is they are selling because it will make you a success too.

Can someone be real here for a second?

Oh, and don't get me started on the perfect sanitized posts some people hide behind on social media. Their families are perfect, their lives are perfect, their businesses are perfect...nobody ever fails.

It's perfectly okay to fail.

Embrace it.

Dropping, Not Pushing!

If you've never been on a podcast before, I would recommend you listen to a few to get an idea of how they work and what other guests do or say. And before saying yes to being a guest on any podcast make sure you understand the rules. Each podcast host is unique and one may allow you to only drop a mention of your product where others may say pushing your product is allowed.

When I'm a guest on someone's podcast, I always make it habit to mention my book and towards the end I'll give the listeners a free gift. Three free audio book chapters of my Sexy Boss

Book. They can either go to my website or text a special word to a code.

www.sexybossinc.com
or Text the word "Sexy" to 72000
(Text service works in USA Only)

If they are already listening on their mobile device, they most likely are going to go to the website or text the word. Texting seems to be what the majority do right now. Try it yourself. I use mobit.com as my "go to" resource for my "text the word" texting service.

Again, I always give that towards the end of the podcast, then I always drop my book or mention something about my company. I'm always bringing it back to what I do every day.

I'm dropping, but I'm <u>not</u> pushing!

It's like I drop it and then go. Most of the time (99%) near to the end of the podcast the host will say, "Okay, Heather, thank you so much for your time. Go ahead and tell us where they can find you."

Pushing a product is the fastest way to turn the audience away. They didn't tune in to be pushed a product, they tuned in to learn. They want to know what you know. They want value. They want to hear how you overcame those failures. They want to know the secrets to your success.

If they want to be pushed a product they would've tuned into the Home Shopping Network or QVC.

Deliver value and content and make your products and services more of an afterthought.

Learn to be subtle. Learn to pepper your talks with mentions here and there so it's more of an "oh, yeah" instead of a "buy from me" situation.

You don't like when your fans, friends and followers push a product or service on social media, or via the telephone or in their daily actions…so why would you try it on a podcast?

Chapter 7

Fitting In, Reaching Out

Not Being A Fit

Out of all the podcasts I've been a guest on all seemed to jell perfectly. But I remember one time there was this guest on my podcast that I had a problem with. It was weird. It was awkward. It wasn't a fit from the get go. And although I probably could have made it fit, this particular guest just wasn't willing to change or alter some of her story to be a fit for me and my listeners. She wasn't willing to shift it. She was stuck and it made the whole podcast go off track. Nope, not a fit at all.

This guest wanted to talk about rape, yet she wasn't shifting or reframing the story to fit the scope of the podcast which was entrepreneurship. It was a major mismatch.

You see, when you get stuck on your story you sometimes become unwilling to, what I call, spin it. Or shift it. Or tweak it. Publicity people call it "reframing". You take your subject and show how it could benefit someone in a totally different field. It works if done properly. If not, "It's a disaster"!

Reframe the story and we can get you on Fox News. Reframe it and now you're on MSNBC. You want to be guest on a podcast you have to be willing to reframe your story to fit the theme. My guest wasn't willing to do that and that made the whole episode feel like a nightmare.

Most entrepreneurs generally when asked to be a guest on a podcast usually make sure that at least they fit. What they are going to talk about, what they are going to be asked is something close to what they do day in and day out in their business. The podcast needs to fit you, your personality, your message, your values, it needs to match your content and is going to reach an audience that you want in the best fashion.

I was asked to be on a podcast with Gary Vaynerchuk. I turned it down. I don't resonate with him. They asked if it was his cursing? I replied, I'm not a big fan of cursing but it wasn't that alone I just don't resonate with his energy. I didn't even want them to try to get me on Gary's podcast. I knew I wasn't a right fit.

But it goes both ways...as, I didn't think his audience would resonate with me. When you don't resonate with someone there is just no way their audience will resonate with you. It just wasn't a right fit. No, I'm not against him. I think he's brilliant and has an awesome brand. It's just how I feel. His brand is not a fit for me.

It's that gut instinct.

Here's my thoughts on cursing…when most of your audience is there to listen to your message they are not there for a curse word lesson. I think it's important to understand for the people is that your message needs to jive with your personality. If you're trying to go after the wrong market, it's like paddling a boat up stream without a paddle. If you're cursing to your market and they don't find that appropriate you're going to have a tough time getting them to stick around to hear all the message.

That's why specifically with Gary, if you don't really resonate with that person and that's their podcast which is part of their personality-focused brand then it's mostly likely their audience isn't going to resonate with you. You're just wasting your time and theirs. Or how about Joe Rogan, I might be able to resonate with him, but I'd have to change my message a little bit to be able to resonate with his audience.

I was a guest on podcast where I knew the person was very spiritual and his audience was too. I had monitored his Facebook posts so I knew a bit about him. So for me to come on the podcast and use Sexy Boss language from my book wasn't going to cut it. Not only would it have tuned him off, but the audience would not have connected.

So I changed my language a bit. Soften it up. Changed my speaking pattern and slowed things down. It was then that I connected nicely with the host and audience.

You have to keep that in mind when you're doing podcasting, or any speaking…engage mentally. If you can't change the way you do things, or the show isn't the right fit…then say no. It's okay.

It's better to say no, then not connect to the audience.

Reaching Out

Networking is a great place to start when looking to be a guest podcaster. There are also services out there that specialize in helping people just like you, find the right connection. Some are free and others you pay a monthly fee.

RadioGuestList.com is a free service. Although they do have a paid version which will keep you updated on which podcasts you can subscribe to and which ones are accepting guests.

You can also pay them to promote you as a guest so they have both promotion sides covered.

LinkedIn is a great resource that will show you all the people that either have a podcast or produced a podcast in some fashion. Just type "podcast" or "podcast host" in the LinkedIn search bar and it will return any inquiry that matches your key terms. From there, you can message those people that fit your criteria.

You can also pay a dedicated Public Relations agency. They go out and find podcasts for you to be on.

I've been paying a service for the last year for a particular package and in return they put me on a set number of podcasts per month. I love it.

Another resource to consider when looking at being a guest on a podcast are good old fashion seminars. With hundreds of seminars covering the gamut of niches the chances of meeting people who can say yes to your request increases with everyone you attend. Although by and large seminars can be expensive to attend and require you to be away from your office for a set number of days.

There's also a ton of Facebook groups about podcasts and for podcast owners that you can join. It's about networking and connecting.

If you don't have the time to network or go to seminars, then go the route of paying for a service. It is worth it.

And if you choose to do so I recommend Natalie Davey at www.ExpertBookers.com - tell her I sent you.

Chapter 8

Evolve and Grow

Being Everywhere!

Now you might be wondering what you should do with the actual podcast. Whether you're the host or the guest the answer is the same...be everywhere with it.

- SoundCloud
- Stitcher
- iHeartRadio
- Google Play
- iTunes
- Amazon
- YouTube

Nowadays, podcasts are everywhere. iTunes is of course what I call the Big Daddy of music hosting and that includes podcasts. Then there's Stitcher and SoundCloud, probably the next two biggest.

The game changer is iHeartRadio, which used to only allow big names and studios to be part of their network of music, talk and sports. Now, they have opened it up to the podcasting world.

So the chances of getting your story to more people is no longer limited to the small scale.

There's Google Play for your Android device. Google is anxious to get that conversation going all you have to do is submit your podcast files.

And then there's Amazon...they do things differently.

Amazon is starting their own podcast world. Unfortunately, it's "pay to play". And, it's a monthly service.

Why pay when you can host your podcasts for free? That's right the service that perfected the mp3 download is the number one "go to" place for uploading your podcasts to. If you said iTunes, you'd be 100% correct.

Although it seems every company out there is jumping on to the podcast platform in some way, even Facebook. Yes, Facebook! They actually want to be your one stop social networking site that offers everything so you never have to look elsewhere.

Podcasting through social media keeps the conversation going. It allows you immediate feedback, access to real-time comments and the ability to share with your friends.

Podcasting is evolving...it's changing...and it's growing.

The new cars hitting the market have the ability to instantly connect with your mobile device or your cloud storage and play your music, your other audio files and yes even your podcasts. Connectability is the key. And podcasting is becoming easier and easier day after day.

If you use services like LibSyn you pay a small monthly fee and your podcast is connected automatically to a multitude of services.

Everywhere.

The days of hiring someone to create the mp3, lay it out, edit it, take the video and render it to mp4 then create images for the marketing are behind us. Doing it yourself to save money, well, there is far better uses for your time and energy. Thank goodness for technology.

The process is almost flawless. As soon as you publish your podcast there are programs now that that automatically convert to any format needed, spit out the proper images and make your life less stressful.

Voilà! Instant authority with your listeners.

Absolutely!

I try to be everywhere with my podcasts in fact… Google me!

Go to Google right now and type…
"Heather Havenwood The Win"

You'll see my website, my iTunes, my Stitcher, my LinkedIn, and my iHeartRadio links plus a whole lot more.

I'm even on YouTube.

Now you might be wondering about LinkedIn and how that works with podcasting. Well, did you know that LinkedIn is now connected with SoundCloud. So now you can listen directly through LinkedIn without being redirected off the site.

Yup, listening just got easier.

Flipping The Business Model

There's a lot of negativity about radio these days. Pundits are like "radio is dying."

Others are downright convinced radio is already dead.

Honestly, I don't know what they are talking about. Sure, it's still the "low hanging fruit" for people who drive in their car. You're really only limited to a few options when driving.

What is changing from my business perspective is sort of what happened to the whole music industry, they're not getting paid enough.

Remember the uproar the music industry had a few years ago?

Everyone was upset.

A radio advertising salesperson a few years ago could make $200,000 easily selling ads and radio sponsorships. That's all shifting. The business models are being flipped around, and some just aren't happy about it. Dead? Nope, not dead! Just different. Believe it or not...radio is actually growing and prospering.

Just not in the old fashioned sense of the word.

Old school radio is changing.

The rules are changing. The models are being flipped.

We get to play with new rules. We don't have to undo anything. I think that's the beauty of it right now. Radio is just adapting to new models and making new technologies work in order to give people more options.

SiriusXM stirred the pot and made commercial free radio a no-brainer for millions across the globe. Sure it was a "pay to play" model, with several different packages, yet it was still radio. But, you weren't limited to an area. Whatever channel you wanted to listened to, it stayed with you everywhere you went.

Yup, the same channel you listen to in San Antonio Texas is the same one you would be listening to in Philadelphia PA. And, for a nominal fee you can expand your SiriusXM listening pleasure to your laptop and mobile device. Hard to do that with conventional radio.

The models are changing every day.

Even podcasts changed how people perceived information now, and where they turn to get it. Just like SiriusXM did for radio people will pay for a never ending supply of brilliant information supplied through podcasts. That information that you're getting from a podcast can supply your business with new ideas, tips, tricks and much needed advice that can help you crank out new sales and give you leverage over your competition.

Podcasts did something else that other mediums didn't. They made you feel that you weren't alone. That you were actually part of the "in" crowd. Like you were sitting with the host and guest sipping coffee and just enjoying the conversation. You felt motivated to go out and try the ideas that were being shared.

Podcasts changed the model to have people feel more connected to real people.

That's exactly how I got started in podcasting...I felt a connection.

Let me tell you that story...

I was actually listening to a podcast about Clickbank.

Incidentally, Clickbank flipped the business model on internet selling and made it easier for entrepreneurs to profit from their products.

Anyway, I thought, "Wow, I can listen to this podcast while I'm driving to the gym once a month and I'll stay up to date."

I didn't have to read their emails anymore, I didn't have to comb through their terms and conditions. I just had to listen.

Well, the more I listened the more the host would showcase different Clickbank users making a good living using the program. I thought it was great. Sometimes, I would talk at the host thinking maybe he could hear me and say, "Oh, I know that guest" or, "oh, I should reach out to that person" or "oh, that guest is kind of cool, he's doing this little trick and getting great results, I should try it."

So I decided to email the host out of the blue.

My email headline to him was, "**I'm <u>NOT</u> a Psycho!**"

In the email I basically said, "Hey, I'd love to be interviewed by you in your podcast". I added a little blurb about me and pressed sent.

He emailed me back. He's email said, "Wow, I never respond to people when they email to the podcast but yours really caught my eye. I have to interview you."

I had never done a podcast before in my life. I didn't know what I was doing. We had a great conversation.

Two weeks later...

I received an email.

It was from a listener from that podcast who heard me and wanted to know more about what I do to help business owners, which turned into a lucrative coaching client.

That was the light bulb moment. I went, "Wait a minute. I just shot the breeze with this guy about something I do every day and made me money. That's crazy. I want more!"

And so I flipped my own model.

I focused 100% on being a great guest. Within 12 months I was on 150 shows, within 18 months it was closer to 250.

Chapter 9

Monetize The Information

Podcasting R.O.I

With every marketing and advertising medium we expect some type of return on investment... podcasting is no different. Podcasting is also unique in that you are leveraging your time for some type of return.

When potential customers call or email you the first thing you typically ask is where did you hear about us, and wait for a response. If they say the phone book, newspaper or even your website you have a general idea of what's working and and what isn't.

However, when you do so many podcasts you have to ask more specific questions. "Thanks for listening to my podcasts do you remember exactly which one peaked your interest?" or "I've been a guest on close to 200 podcasts can you narrow down the exact one you heard?"

Personally, all my current clients have come from me being a guest on podcasts. So when you try to factor out the return on investment...a podcast is a great leverage of your time.

But here's the important thing...a podcast doesn't have the limited shelf life of say a webinar, Facebook ad, radio ad, TV ad or even a social media post. Nope...a podcast as longevity. Listeners are constantly discovering podcasts and so one you recorded a year ago may have just gotten heard today.

I will tell you this...that prior to me to being a guest on the many many podcasts, the traffic to my website was slim at best. I spent gobs of money to have the website built and then did Facebook ads. Now fast forward through all the podcasts and I'm getting thousands of visitors to my website without paying the big Facebook ad spend.

How do I know? Well, I watch my analytics and I can see all the links that people are clicking in from to find me. No paid ads, no Facebook boosting, no social media advertising whatsoever. No paid media. Nope!

The return on investment is strictly from podcasts.

I know a lot of people who spend tons of money on Facebook ads and had they just considered for a moment the advantages of podcasting and what it could do for them, their conversions would be so much higher.

Just think about it. If I'm doing an ad on Facebook and then I post my ad on my Facebook page, which really is kind of strange, but let's say I do, what are the chances of your audience sharing it? Slim right?

But what if I posted a picture accompanied by a description and I said on this really cool podcast is a cool marketing dude, the chances of someone sharing is much higher.

Or…

"Oh, I'm about to listen to this podcast. Go check it out yourself."

Or…

"Hey, just listen to it, it's really cool. I learned three things."

Or…

"Hey, I was just on this podcast. I share three ways to… It's really awesome. You should go listen to it."

All those examples are still better than... *"Hey, here's a great advertisement."*

That's the beauty of podcasts, you are engaging people in your story then sharing that story on social media to keep the conversation going. And that is how you increase your ROI through guesting.

Tuning In To The Right Information

The benefit of a podcast is being able to just enjoy someone else's conversation. You're learning from them, and I think that it has more compelling reaction than just listening to rehearsed questions.

That's the very reason I don't rehearse. I never know the questions I am going to be asked.

I think some people need to have an idea of what's coming. Maybe it helps them with the flow of things. Hey I'm okay with that. But, the questions shouldn't be studied and prepped.

If you ask for an outline of sorts than you are prepared. But never ask for the exact questions.

I tell all my guests, "Hey this is just an outline. If we happen to move off it or cover additional material, just roll with it." I never say, "This is how it goes."

If you're listening to a podcast and you know every single question that they are going to ask, it's going to be boring. Even big companies like Vogue don't want to be boring. They have it figured out. They do their famous 73 questions. They go around asking amazing actors and actresses the long list of questions. Yet, they always seem to ask unique questions geared toward the individual.

Imagine if Vogue asked the same questions to every different actor or actress? After a while you would know what they would say and when guests like Nicole Kidman or Jennifer Aniston answered…you'd be "Oh, I bet I know what they are going to say."

Same goes for podcasts. I think it would become really boring when listening to a podcast if all the questions where the same for every guest.

You want to be <u>entertained</u>…not be bored to death.

I find sometimes the marketing that entrepreneurs post to their Facebook, or Twitter or even LinkedIn can equate to information overload. Sometimes I just need to tune it out and tune into and listen to a podcast. I need to focus on hearing someone else's words so I don't have to read the constant postings of everyone's so-called perfect life.

That's right, social media can be a bit overwhelming sometimes. Everyone's posts are sanitized to make the poster look like a Nobel Peace Prize winner. With a podcast I can actually listen and know the guest is human and has flaws and failures. They are real. The conversation is real.

Another thing that makes listeners tune in…is your bio.

Yup, that introduction that you give the host that tells a bit about you.

The mistake I see way too many guests doing is they create a long bio. You know, nothing screams OMG <u>boring</u> than listening to someone rattle on about another's accomplishments. Huge mistake!

Imagine being a host and reading your guest's bio, "Hi we have Rob with us today, and Rob is…blah, blah, blah, yada, yada, yada." On and on and on and on and on. And you're thinking, "Come on, who cares about his 6 kids and a dog...screw it, I will just talk to him."

Hey, sorry, long bios don't work...and they turn people off. Sure you have a lot of accomplishments you want to showcase, but seriously, most people just want to hear your story not your resume.

Do yourself a favor and listen to Jimmy Kimmel or Rush Limbaugh or even Howard Stern. How do they introduce people? A simplified shortened bio, right? Listen, they'll be like, "We got Rob on the line. What's going on Rob?" Sure he might have some book that is super awesome or a killer website. But instead of saying any of that, they continue on with, "Hey, Rob".

These hosts are experts at being conversational. And when people listen in, they will think you're such the cool expert too. It's entertaining. Not boring. A good host doesn't need to use the bio as he/she can pull it apart and fish it out later during the podcast. So instead of the boring resume, maybe they mix it by saying, "It says here Rob, you have like 6000 kids, that's interesting. How's that going for you? Let's talk about that. How did you do that while be an entrepreneur?"

So as a podcast guest your job is to make your bio somewhat interesting without boring the host or listener. The host's job is to turn that bio into something interesting during the podcast. Your job, as a guest, is to entertain.

And never, ever write your bio in 3rd person. As in, "I, followed by your name...."

Yeah, it happens. Hosts are so busy they sometimes are handed bios at the last minute and don't always have time to review it. So they start announcing the guest and wham-o they have an "I" in front of their name and the host just read that. Ugh!

As a listener when you tune into a podcast and the host is reading a long bio or one that is written in 3rd person, I bet you won't be listening for too long.

Chapter 10

Getting Your Ducks
In A Row

Make It Easy For Them To Say "YES" To You!

There are so many people out there that have great material, but they make it difficult to find, so they never get selected as a guest on a podcast. So if you're thinking about being a guest on podcasts you have to make it easy for the host to say "Yes" to you.

The big question I get from entrepreneurs looking to get on podcasts is, "How do I get selected?"

My response…
"There's a couple of ways…here's how."

Then I proceed to share the ways with whomever is asking.

The first one, and this is very crucial, is setting up your media page to make it easy for others to say yes to you. In the marketing world we would call this "creating a funnel." Funnels are the process of moving a prospect to a buyer. In the case of your media pages it works to make it easier to get invited as guest.

In any kind of media, specifically podcast media, you've got to make it easy for people to do business with you. So, let me tell you what not to do.

Don't hoop jump!

If you do actually get selected to get on a podcast and they request your information, don't send them everything separately in different attachments. One email directs them to your Dropbox, another to your website and another to an audio file. Hoop jumping.

You have to understand that the podcast host doesn't have all this time to go looking for your information. Their job as host is already tied up in creating and promoting the podcast, now you want them to jump through hoops trying to piece together your information from various links, pages and resources? No, no, no, no.

There's all these pieces, and you've got to learn to make it easy for others to assemble the puzzle. Make it easy for people to say "Yes" to you.

The way to make it easy...create a media page.

It sounds simple, but I can't tell you how many people mess it up.

I suggest you either "steal" mine. Okay not really steal it, but copy it so that all you have to do is remove my information and then insert your information in the blanks. Or hire me to help you and I'll create it for you. Many just opt to hire me, as I've gotten the process down to a science and I know what works. I make it easy for people to do business with you. Which, is probably why I receive so many messages that go like this...

"Thank you so much for doing this. It makes it easy for me and my team to do business with you."

My media page in case you wish to copy is...
www.heatherhavenwood.com/media

The first thing you might notice when going to my page is I make it easy for people to do business with me. I give them choices. Various size images, long and short bio's, everything in one place.

Maybe you heard of companies hiring PR agencies at monthly rates of $3,000, $4,000, $6,000 or more to be pitched to the media. Well, that's fine if they want to throw away money. When you are paying these prices and not getting the publicity you want you will feel like you're getting the "runaround".

Is it the agencies fault or the person wanting to a guest? Most times it's the guest because they don't have all their "ducks in a row" (not having their media pages set up, not having everything in one place to pull from, not make it easier).

That's what we call being a "pain in the butt".

Don't be a pain in the butt!

Be an easy person/company to to do business with. Give them a reason to say...
"You've made it so easy for me, let's do it again."

When you go to my media page, I mentioned earlier, there are choices. What I mean by choices is I have elements that make it easy for the media to grab easily and effortlessly.

I have various size photos which include high and low resolution head shots, body shots and book covers and other images that can be easily downloaded.

I also have a long and short bio, which can be easily copied and pasted. Easy!

I make it simple because the podcast host usually gives the task to an assistant who might be instructed to obtain the information for their boss. Now it's all in one place and the assistant is happy. The host is happy.

On the bottom of my media page I have what I call my online business. It has all my URL's. Why? Well at the end of almost every podcast, the host usually asks something like this, "Where can people find you?' or "What other stuff do you have?"

The media page online business URL's have the descriptions ready and make it easy for the host to share you with the audience.

You have got to be easy to do business with! It sounds so simple, so common sense.

As a host, I can't tell you how many times I've done business with professional experts, I'm talking major professional experts in their field and they're literally, "Oh, I don't know where my bio is" or "I only have this one small headshot" or "let me find that Google doc". And I'm like, "now I've got to go put that in a folder somewhere." You know what I mean? It's the little stuff.

Pitch Yourself

Now I do use several companies to pitch for me. But honestly, it's a relatively small monthly budgeted amount. I keep them around because they are consistent. They know my criteria and continuously look out for me. I also pitch myself.

In fact, the majority of guest spots are from me pitching myself to podcasts. And all from emails, that go something like this...

"Hi, my name is Heather, I would like for you to consider having me as guest on your podcast. I've taken a look at your podcast and I think I'm a great fit. Here's why..."

Then, I'll add...

"You know, here's a potential title of the podcast I could do..."

And, I add a quick title.

Then before sending the email I make sure I include...
"Here's my media page..."

I then add my media page URL into the email.

Once they open the email and click on the media page they know within seconds if I'm a good fit or not.

It's an easy process. And that's how you should always look at it. If you're not making it easy for someone to say "Yes" to you, then you should start, now!"

There's something that happens when you start pitching yourself to bloggers, media outlets and podcasters...when you pitch yourself that's when you really start to understand the business.

If you go to my website, you'll see I'm actually on KXAN/NBC which is a local Austin station. Yes, I pitched them. I was proud of that. I got on TV myself. I actually called the producer and said, "This is what I would like to talk about". I gave him 3 options on titles. He picked. I said, "Great'. The show turned out fantastic.

You can see the TV segment on my media page www.heatherHavenwood.com/media

When you pitch yourself you learn what people want. I highly suggest you do it. Sell you!

You can opt for a service if you wish. And I highly suggest you learn to sell you!

Chapter 11

Branding You

Own Your Brand

Let's go back to media pages for bit. You see there are a great deal of people, entrepreneurs especially, who speak for a living and have absolutely no media pages on their website.

To be honest, I didn't always have a media page either. It wasn't until recently (about 1 year ago) I saw the value in using a media page. That's when more and more people starting reaching out to me. They would say...

"Hey, I want you to be on my show!"

Then they would use the wrong image pulled from one of my old social media pages. Oh, it was horrible.

Listen, your image is your brand. And you need to be able to control what is being pushed out online.

A dedicated media page on your website is going to give people the right photos of you, that you choose.

When you're starting out as a guest maybe your mind isn't always focused on the big picture. I get that. However, when someone uses the wrong image of you that's not flattering in anyway, it might be upsetting. Trust me, I know.

I've been down that road...it's not pretty.

"Where'd you get that...image?"

To which they reply...

"Oh, my assistant went to Google and typed your name and that's what she found."

Hmm, no!

My response...

"Okay, great. But please go to this page and go get my image there."

What I find is that some people just aren't used to guests having media pages. So they have assistants looking in all the wrong places.

They just aren't used to it.

A few days prior to writing this chapter, I was on a skype call recording a podcast I had just wrapped up and they asked, "Will you send me your image?" I reply, "Yeah, it's on my media page, I've shared it with via email, but let me share it again."

I enter the URL of my media page into the Skype chat feature.

They want to know why they can't just pull the image off of Facebook.

On my site I share high resolution pictures of myself that have the best clarity. When I state high resolution I mean any picture with a 300dpi or more quality.

The pictures you pull from Facebook although might be uploaded as high resolution, Facebook downgrades them to 72dpi for space savings. So the image you are pulling from Facebook is not high resolution in any way, shape or form.

So when you are dealing with media personal you never know what they will be doing with your image. They might take you image and make it bigger...I mean really blow it up bigger. If the image is low resolution when they enhance it...it will look all pixelated and horrible.

I mentioned this before, give them choices. I give them options of my pictures to choose from. A headshot, a body shot and maybe an action shot.

My image is my brand, so I need to control how it's being used and where. If they (the media) are using an image that doesn't convey my brand I let them know and give them options to change it.

It's that simple.

Controlling and owning your brand also includes giving people the right information about you. So I include a one sheet on my media page.

What's a one sheet?

In a nutshell, a one sheet is basically a sheet of page that contains the highlights of who I am, what I do and my short bio.

It contains my name and lots of bullet points of the things I believe are my strengths.

- Build Your Business
- Build Your Wealth
- Live Your Dream
- How To Succeed
- Business Coaching
- Radical Growth
- Money Freedom

Then it has six areas of talks I normally like to focus on.

✓ Marketing
✓ Sell Like A Boss
✓ Solo Entrepreneurship
✓ Communications
✓ Information Marketing
✓ Producing Results

It's all on a downloadable PDF that anyone can open or email. Your one sheet also acts as a way to weed out the podcasts that just don't fit. By listing what your strengths are, you are telling people "hey, if we can work together, great, this is what I talk about, if not, no worries."

Want to check my one sheet out? Go to my website, then my media page and under the NBC interview you'll see a link to click on my media kit one sheet.

www.HeatherHavenwood.com/media

Your strengths will be different than mine. And that's good. Maybe your concentration is on: Social Media, Search Engine Optimization, Publishing or Ghostwriting, etc.

You don't want to be invited on a podcast about sewing if you have zero experience in the sewing field. No, you want to hone in on only those podcasts you have experience in and can share your stories and bond with the audience.

Your branding needs to be able to convey authority while also making it easy for podcasters to say yes to working with you.

Your Bio

Let's talk about your bio! Do you even have one? If you do, how long is it? I bet it is too long. Remember, you bio is not your resume.

There's a lot of people who put way too much stuff on their bios. What they should is simplify. Take their long bio and shortened it down to less than a paragraph. Remember time is money, and listeners don't have time to be listening to all your accomplishments. So shortened the bio.

Now in the event that you wish to show off your accomplishment you can have a long and short bio. The podcast host can choose which one to use. In most cases it will be the shorter one.

Your long bio is something that the podcast host can include on their blog, which gives more information about you that might not be on the podcast.

On television and even cable shows the interview process is quick.

Typically, the host wants a one sentence bio for the podcast. Something like, "Hi everyone, this is Heather and I'm interviewing Rob, and Rob is the co-author of this book..."

Here we go!

It's really quick. First name, last name, name of book or business...and go!

Podcasts are not as quick and allow a little more room for your details.

"This is Heather, I'm with Rob A...he's an expert on...his most recent book is called...let's get started."

Your bio can be a little longer on podcasts but shorter on TV.

Chapter 12

Making Sure You're Heard

Prepping

To be prepped, or not be prepped...as a podcasting guest. You know that's a concern for some. We talked about the fear of not knowing in a previous chapter, and how that fear can stifle our answers and make us sound stiff and unsure. But we also talked about improv'ing and learning how to be calm and cool and use our wit to come up with quick responses.

Sure I understand the whole, "I don't want to get blindsided" part. Been there, done that.

So, here's what I suggest...

When I'm pitching myself to be a guest on someone's podcast I give the host the option of a meet and greet. It's a short phone call or video conference where I can get to know them, ask them questions and get a feel for what the podcast is all about. And, it goes both ways. The host can quickly learn more about me, my personality and can gauge my comfort level to the material. It's simply a meet and greet.

The meet and greet, to me, helps alleviate any doubts I might have, allows me get to know the host a bit better, and prepares me on how to adjust better to his/her audience.

Another thing I would suggest you do is go online and send a direct chat message to them. It could be... "It's nice to meet you. I'm so excited about being on your podcast as a guest. Can you tell me more about it? Can you tell me more about your audience? Can you tell me why you started the podcast and what your overall intention is?"

Most podcasters will open up and tell you.

"Well, I started because…"

"The audience is…"

"I really want to help others because…"

The more you know about the podcast, the host or the audience the more comfortable you'll be and your answers will sound clearer, more articulated and spontaneous.

Never assume as a guest you fully understand the audience without doing a meet and greet or asking questions prior to the interview in the "greenroom".

As a host when I reach out to guests to do a meet and greet I'm surprised by their reactions. I'm finding that the majority of guests have never been prepped, have no clear idea what the podcast is about and some really have no clear story to share.

I remember as guest I had a meet and greet with a podcast host and he was like, "Well, usually the people who are listening it's like 60% men and 40% women. They mainly own a digital agency and they're looking to grow their business. Got it?"

Ah, nope!

Apparently, the host really didn't know his audience and as it sounded probably was never asked the question of who is audience really was.

If you were a speaker and you walked on stage, wouldn't you like to know if you're talking to a thousand people who are in MLM or a thousand corporate owners?

Same goes for podcasting. You want to know the audience you are speaking to, right?

Can You Hear Me Now?

Cell phones are great. Don't you agree? They allow us to connect with anyone no matter where we are. Unfortunately, for podcasting they have their drawbacks.

Recently, I had an amazing expert on my podcast and I had to give him hell. It was a tough call, because I knew how famous he was. He's given thousands of hours of presentations all over the world. And here he was on my podcast using his cell phone. I was livid. The sound quality was horrible. It was like being in static echo chamber. I seriously considered stopping the podcast.

Finally, I asked him, "Are you on a cell phone?"

To which he replied that he was.

So I responded, "Where's your landline, or microphone, do you know what Skype is?"

Sadly, he didn't have a landline, or a microphone or knew how to use Skype.

What? Why?

Okay, I get the whole not having a landline thing.

Skype is available as a download for every type of computer. Don't use Skype on Wi-Fi. You must be plugged directly in. If you try to record over Wi-Fi, the signal will go in and out and quality of the show will be undesirable.

And frankly investing in a microphone will be one of the smartest decision you can make when it comes to your podcasting career. It's just that important.

What I use today for my podcasts is a condenser microphone with a big swivel arm complete with a mixer. But that's not how I started.

My "go to" mike is a Yeti. Actually, it's called a Blue Yeti and it has a USB connector that plugs right into your computer. Plus, you can plug your headphones straight into it which eliminates feedback noise.

That's really all you need. Keep it simple!

I did over 120 podcasts just with my Yeti, then I stepped it up and got the mixer and swivel mike and went crazy. Funny thing is, I still prefer the Yeti.

You don't need a lot to get started as a guest podcaster. Nope! A brand new Yeti might set you back $100-$150. You don't need to buy special headphones. It's that simple. Just make sure you can use headphones that do not have a mic on them.

The high tech stuff…nope! You don't need it. Not to get started.

Skype, a good mic and some headphones attached to your desktop or laptop computer and a direct connection online, no Wi-Fi… that's all you need. Oh, and a quiet area.

You can't be guesting from Starbucks. You can't have kids running around in the background. The dog should be outside. And the ringer to the landline and your cellphone turned off. No noise. No distractions. Just a quiet closed environment.

I know some will say Starbucks is great for getting work done, for meeting clients and guzzling those Venti coffees…but it's lousy for podcasting.

It's not quiet at all. And all the noise and people in the background talking can be heard on the podcast. It's very distracting.

Going back to the expert who used his cell phone. Every time he would move the phone across his ears you would hear the shuffling sound...the hush-hush-hush-hush. It's annoying and what we call that in the industry "bad audio".

And quite honestly, I don't know anyone who really likes to listen to "bad audio". They'll turn it off.

A friend of mine who's a brilliant YouTube video guy says that, "the video can be crap, but the audio has to be awesome".

Maybe you've experienced that too. The video can be grainy and distorted, but if the audio is horrible you just turn the program off. Audio has got to be crystal clear.

Now, if you don't like Skype for some reason you can use Zoom.us which a fantastic audio or video recording platform.

Oh, and lest we forget...a strong direct internet connection is always important if you are using Skype, Zoom or any other platform on our desktop, laptop or internet device.

Wi-Fi is basically a short radio signal that can be disrupted or interfered with that might cause you to lose your connection to the web.

My advice: connect your laptop directly to your router so essentially you are dialed in and free of the signal interruptions.

Even if you have to go to RadioShack and buy a 100ft router cable to be connected...just do it.

Final thoughts...

Never leave podcasting to chance...make sure you're heard.

About The Authors

Heather Havenwood – CEO of Havenwood Worldwide, LLC and Chief Sexy Boss, is a serial entrepreneur and is regarded as a top authority on internet marketing, business strategies and marketing. Since marketing her first online business in 1999, bringing together clients and personal coaches, she has played an active role in the online marketing world since before most even had a home computer. www.HeatherHavenwood.com

Rob Anspach – founder of Anspach Media, is an experienced Social Media Strategist, SEO Expert, Author, Speaker and Trust Creator who can transform and monetize your brand. Rob works inside corporations across the globe, helping companies generate new revenue and capture online business. www.AnspachMedia.com

Other Books By The Authors

Heather Havenwood

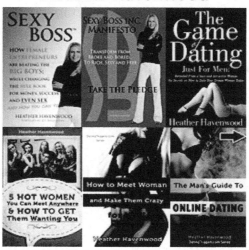

Rob Anspach

Available On Amazon

Resources

DatingTriggers.com ==> Site for men to learn how to attract and communicate with women

SuccessMagnetSeminar.com ==> The 2013 Las Vegas Seminar with Joe Sugarman, Joe Polish, John Carlton, Jon Benson and Heather Havenwood

SexyBossInc.com ==> Site for the print and audio versions of the SEXY BOSS™ book

CoachWithHeather.com ==> Interested in doubling your sales and tripling your time off? Get on a Discovery Call with Heather Today!

SexyBossShow.com ==> Podcast on I-tunes for Women Entrepreneurship

ExpertBookers.com ==> an elite service helping you get booked as a guest on podcasts

AnspachMedia.com ==> helping professionals build trust with their audience through the use of online marketing, content creation and publishing

Working With Heather

Now you too can work with Heather Havenwood and get coaching from the best.

Dear Friend and fellow Entrepreneur,

I'm currently looking for just a small handful of "dream" clients that I can personally coach and help bring in **massive windfalls for, starting RIGHT NOW.**

If you're the kind of <u>passionate, committed, entrepreneurial client I'm looking for,</u> I will personally work with you one-on- one in your business to help you double, triple, or maybe even quadruple your revenue for the next 12 months.

Here's the deal:
I've just cleared out a handful of spots in my calendar to personally work with a few serious entrepreneurs who want to take their business to the next level.

And if you qualify, I'm going to offer you a 100% FREE consultation and strategy session with me by phone or Skype.

There is NO charge for this and there's NO catch.

If you enjoy the conversation and get value from it, we can discuss working together long term.

And if you feel I've wasted your time in our conversation, I'll even send you a check for $150.00 as compensation.

Either way, you come out ahead.

HeatherHavenwood.com

Rip Heather Off!

Want to see an ideal Media Page?

One that will help all podcast show hosts say YES to you easily and effortlessly?

Go Here!

www.HeatherHavenwood.com/media

Interested in Interviewing Heather on your NEW Podcast?

She is always a YES!

Please fill out the form for an Interview Request.

www.HeatherHavenwood.com/media

Share This Book!

I mean it!

Tell your friends all about this book.

Share where you bought it.

Share it at lunch!

Share it at the gym!

Share it on the beach!

Share it on social media.

Share it using this hashtag...

#PowerGuesting

Made in the USA
Las Vegas, NV
12 May 2023

71959882R00069